The Power to SIZZLE

Transformational POWER Thoughts for Creating the
Life You Want

Cheryl Wood

The Power to SIZZLE – Transformational POWER
Thoughts for Creating the Life You Want

Published by Cheryl Wood Empowers
8787 Branch Avenue, Suite 213
Clinton, MD 20735
301-395-7589
www.cherylwoodempowers.com

Cheryl Wood Empowers is committed to empowering girls
and women to make fearless moves to create the reality
they want in their lives. The company reflects the
philosophy established by the founder: Embrace your
personal power to visualize and achieve your personal,
career, or business goals; boldly step outside of your
comfort zone, take calculated risks, and remove self-
limiting beliefs to reach your greatest potential.

Cover Design by Nibrima Branding & Design

Published in the United States of America

ISBN #978-1-4675-8124-0

Self-Help/General

Other Books by Cheryl Wood available on Amazon:

How I Flatlined and Woke Up in 45 Days –
A Guide to Empowered Living

The GlamourLESS Side of Entrepreneurship –
What They DIDN'T Tell You About Being A
Woman In Business

Website:
www.CherylWoodEmpowers.com

Connect with Cheryl Wood on social media:
Facebook.com/CherylEmpowers
Twitter.com/CherylEmpowers
YouTube.com/CherylEmpowers
Linkedin.com/in/CherylEmpowers
Instagram/CherylEmpowers

Dedicated to the many mentors, coaches, fans and supporters who celebrate the authentic "Sizzle" I have created in my life in order to become the best version of myself and, in turn, positively impact the lives of others who are touched by my message and my journey.

Cheryl Wood

CONTENTS

Introduction

"Your ultimate success and ability to create your own Sizzle in life is defined by your thoughts. Every day, choose thoughts that are positive and progressive, and witness the shift in your life." (Cheryl Wood)

So, what is Sizzle? Sizzle is the unique space you carve out for yourself in the world and the un-duplicable mark you leave based on your gifts and talents that no one can take from you. That means, every person reading this book has The Power to SIZZLE.

Truthfully, as a young, African-American girl raised in poverty in the projects of Baltimore City, the product of a single-parent household, I never expected to have the word "Sizzle" show-up in my life. If anything, I expected just the opposite. As I observed my surroundings growing up – mostly crime, violence, poverty, and lack of educational resources – I presumed I was destined for very little success in my life. But the one glimmer of hope came from a woman I respected as the epitome of belief: my mother. Her constant belief that things would work out, that she could somehow create a solution to every challenge she faced, and the fortitude that she did not have to become a product of her environment moved me to start believing I had a choice in the type of life I could create for myself.

I never saw my mother cave into the pressure she clearly faced as a single mother raising three young children on a minimal salary as a public school cafeteria manager. I never saw her express disgust or lack of willpower to find solutions even when she didn't know how she was going to feed us, pay a utility bill, afford school clothes, or pay for repairs to our used, barely-running Chevrolet Nova that took us to and from "only the necessary" places. My mother was (and still is) by far one of the most inspirational women in my life. She instilled in me hope that thru hard work, persistence, determination, loyalty, and trustworthiness, I could accomplish anything. She was the first female influence in my life who taught me the power of shifting my thoughts to create the reality I wanted. And, now, as a mother myself I instill that same training in my three children so they understand the power they have to become, do, or accomplish anything they put their minds to.It's so true that shifting your mindset can shift your life. And the only way to shift your mindset is to shift your thoughts. Your thoughts can either motivate and energize you to get what you want in life or hinder you and keep you stuck where you are right now in life. Granted, that's not to say that because you start thinking positive thoughts right now that your goals, aspirations and dreams will miraculously come to fruition tomorrow.

Let's face it, you have to put in the work for what you say you want. And reaching the stars is going to require a lot of climbing. It takes time to SIZZLE. It's a process like anything else. And it's a daily journey that will have highs and lows. But the guarantee is that as you shift your thoughts to POWER thoughts – positive, empowering thoughts that refuel you to keep pushing towards your big dream – you will become more determined than ever not to throw in the towel. One of the best pieces of advice I ever heard was, "You only fail when you stop trying." (Bob Marley)

As you delve into the 150 POWER Thoughts in this book, allow each thought to sink-in and transform who you are, how you think, and what you believe you can accomplish!

150 POWER Thoughts

for Creating the Life You Want

POWER Thought #1

You cannot walk confidently in your present if you're still stuck in your past – dwelling on everything that has gone wrong, who hurt you, and what you have not accomplished. Today is the day to abandon past insecurities, fears and doubts, and instead embrace new belief in yourself that you have what it takes to get what you want in life starting NOW.

POWER Thought #2

Stop waiting for validation or permission. No other individual and no amount of accolades can convince you that you are good enough -- that's an inside job. It's all on YOU! Repeat this on a daily basis because you deserve to create your own reality then grant yourself permission to dream bigger, play bigger, and expect to achieve the results you work hard for.

POWER Thought #3

Fail, get up & try again; Fail, get up & try again; Fail, get up & try again. Don't give up because everything isn't going your way. Instead, view every failure as another clue of what not to do and, thus, a step in the right direction. Keep picking yourself up and dusting off to discover creative new ways, new ideas, and new strategies to get to your ultimate goal.

POWER Thought #4

Regardless of how many conferences, workshops, or training sessions you attend, how many thousands of dollars you spend on learning products, and how many coaches you hire... until you firmly believe in your gifts and EXECUTE on what's already in your arsenal you will keep getting the same results. Starting today, utilize what you already have and know to get unstuck.

POWER Thought #5

Your voice and your story deserve to be heard. Commit to telling your story and letting your light shine brightly so your unique gift can become a beacon of inspiration for someone else. Refuse to abandon your gift or dim your light because you're afraid you won't succeed, because you think you're inadequate, or even because the brightness of your light makes some people feel uncomfortable. Instead, become as bright as possible!

POWER Thought #6

You've thought about it, dreamed about it, lost sleep over it, woke up in the middle of the night brainstorming on it, written a notepad of ideas about it, posted about it on social media, told your friends about it, and prayed about it -- so now is the time for you to stop procrastinating. Now is the time to move forward and EXECUTE it! No matter how long you wait, the big dream you want for your life will never fall into your lap. You must be intentional about finding ways to make it happen.

POWER Thought #7

Your ability to thrive in life is directly linked to your willingness to develop and manifest critical "success" characteristics -- confidence vs. arrogance, humility vs. timidity, inspiration vs. manipulation, and growth vs. stagnation. Every day, grade your personal performance and make room for improvement.

POWER Thought #8

Never forget that you are not defined by what you do or the "title" you hold. You are defined by your unique abilities, qualities, characteristics, talents, values, and principles that directly position you to live up to your fullest potential while finding ways to serve and support others in reaching their fullest potential.

POWER Thought #9

Now is not the time to shrink back from your purpose. Keep taking steps to discover what fulfills you and nurtures your spirit and then share that with the world. Remain determined to boldly walk in your purpose and create a living legacy.

POWER Thought #10

Instead of losing sleep over how far you have to go in my journey, choose to celebrate how far you've come. Choose to reflect on the lessons learned, the experiences gained, the relationships developed, and the lives you have impacted.

POWER Thought #11

Success is not a secret formula that only certain people have access to. Success is having the boldness to create your own opportunities, the courage to do the things that make you uncomfortable, and to keep your eyes focused on the ultimate prize no matter what obstacles knock you down temporarily. Success is staying in the race and crawling your way to the finish line because you never know what's around the next corner in your journey unless you keep moving.

POWER Thought #12

Do not be afraid to surround yourself with people who have more knowledge, experience, resources, and success than you do. It takes nothing from you and it does not mean you don't have anything in common with those who are already soaring. Rather, it means you are wise enough to position yourself with those who can teach you, guide you, and elevate you.

POWER Thought #13

Vow not to spend time sweating the "small stuff" and exerting unnecessary energy on things you cannot control. Instead, focus your energy on the things you CAN change and improve in your life.

POWER Thought #14

A positive outlook, regardless of how bleak the circumstances may look, is a choice. Each day, start by shifting your thoughts to develop and demonstrate an internal gratitude for all the blessings you have. When you shift your thoughts your actions will follow suit and you will begin to create the reality you desire.

POWER Thought #15

When you refuse to share your life experiences and tell your story, you are obstructing your legacy. Instead of discounting the impact your story can have on someone else's life, tell your story loud and proud!

POWER Thought #16

If you really want to achieve success and prosperity you must add Persistence to your Prayers, Follow Through to your Faith, Intention to your Inspiration, and Movement to your Motivation. Nothing will happen until you persistently follow through on your intentions and make constant moves towards pursuing what you say you want.

POWER Thought #17

There are scores of people who are too scared to pursue their dream, so they might try to talk you out of living yours. When they come your way with doubt and negativity, just say NO – NO to changing your plans, NO to being infected with negative vibes, and NO to dwindling your desire to press forward.

POWER Thought #18

Repeatedly ask yourself: Do I choose to be held hostage by fear or will I permit myself to be enlightened by hope and possibilities? Your possibilities in life will be as big as you make room for. Stop playing small!

POWER Thought #19

In order to overcome challenges, setbacks, and roadblocks in your journey to success, focus more on where you want to be than where you are now. The circumstances you're experiencing now are only temporary, but you have the power to create solutions to those circumstances and create a new reality.

POWER Thought #20

Whenever people pour into your life, find ways to pour into someone else's life realizing that your greatest blessings come when you intentionally create a balance between receiving blessings and extending yourself to serve others.

POWER Thought #21

You will succeed, not necessarily because you are destined to, but because you are determined to. To be determined means you conclusively and authoritatively make the decision to achieve your desired outcome no matter what.

POWER Thought #22

Sometimes you will feel like a "little fish" in a "big ocean" whose voice isn't being heard as you're pursuing your dream, but don't fret… it doesn't mean you're not making a difference and changing lives. Just when you think no one is looking and listening, they are. Embrace the humble beginnings that get you closer to your BIG dream! And never stop moving.

POWER Thought #23

Refuse to be a victim to negative self-talk. It is time to UPGRADE your inner dialogue and speak greatness into your life. When you upgrade your inner dialogue it positively impacts your words, thoughts, beliefs and actions, and makes you aware of your personal power to achieve anything you set your mind to.

POWER Thought #24

Don't slow down. Don't lose focus.
Don't diminish your roar for success.
You will get scrapes and bruises along
the journey but what doesn't break you
will only make you stronger, bolder, and
more determined than ever to finish the
race.

POWER Thought #25

Verbalize and Visualize your big dream. Talk about your dream as often as possible to keep it alive. Connect the verbalization to visualization. Think about what it will look like and feel like to achieve your dream. Keeping your dream alive in your mind will give you the boost to never turn back.

POWER Thought #26

Avoid being a bystander in your own potential success story. Get moving, create a plan, and implement the plan. While you're waiting for the right moment, someone else is executing and living their dream!

POWER Thought #27

There is no need to follow anyone else's footsteps - create your own! Leave your unique footprint on the world by using your voice, story, gifts, and talents to live out loud.

POWER Thought #28

Commit to being committed. Put in the work for your big dream, no matter how challenging it gets, with the understanding that your efforts will not be in vain. You WILL achieve your desired outcome as long as you refuse to quit!

POWER Thought #29

Today, create reasons and avoid excuses. You have everything it takes to achieve the best version of you as long as you make it a non-optional decision.

POWER Thought #30

Change doesn't happen, Change is created. Decide how bad you want to create a new story for your life and start creating change today. Remember, small steps lead to huge feats.

POWER Thought #31

Every day that you wake up with the mental attitude to WIN, you put yourself one step closer to winning. Silence your inner critic and press on full-steam ahead to test the limits of what you can achieve if you just try.

POWER Thought #32

"A mind focused on doubt and fear cannot focus on the journey to victory." (M.Jones). What is your mind focused on today? Are you focused on whether or not you think you have the strength to persist or is it focused on what's most important – how amazing it will feel when you cross the finish line?

POWER Thought #33

Admit what you don't know and then go
learn it! Your ultimate success in
achieving any goal is linked to your
willingness to remain teachable and
keep learning. Allow new knowledge to
push you into your next level of
greatness.

POWER Thought #34

Repeat the following oath, "Today, I will be productive not busy. I will focus more of my time on executing good ideas versus simply thinking about good ideas. I will proactively do the things that produce results."

POWER Thought #35

When you find your passion, jump in with both feet. Don't cheat yourself out of what could be a life altering experience. And don't wait for perfection. Instead, figure out the answers as you go along which will result in a journey filled with discovery and priceless opportunities. You owe it to yourself to explore the possibilities.

POWER Thought #36

The only way to get to where you want to be is to get COMFORTABLE being UNCOMFORTABLE. When you place yourself in the path of unfamiliarity, discomfort, and fear... you begin to push the envelope and identify what you are truly capable of accomplishing in life. Become unstoppable!

POWER Thought #37

Don't stay shut in a box – stretch
yourself – to meet new people, make
new connections, travel to new places.
When you have the boldness to step
outside of the norm and beyond
boundaries, you discover who you are
and how much life really has to offer
you.

POWER Thought #38

You don't need MORE to step into your God-given greatness -- MORE time, MORE planning, MORE education, MORE validation -- you just need to get started. Step into what you've been destined to do without anymore hesitation.

POWER Thought #39

Each day that you wake up, you control your outlook and focus for the day. You control what you accomplish or don't accomplish. No one has the power to hold you back but from your desired achievements except you!

POWER Thought #40

To BELIEVE that you are destined to succeed means you refuse to stay down-for-the-count when challenges arise. Dust yourself off, treat the wounds, and start working on the next step in your master plan. Continue supporting your belief in your ability to win by staying in action.

POWER Thought #41

Your personal success depends on you –
knowing decisively which direction
you're headed in and having unshakable
faith that you are capable of reaching
any port no matter how turbulent the sea
or how distant the destination!

POWER Thought #42

The moment you make success less
about you and more about impacting
someone else's life, you will begin to
soar beyond your greatest expectations.

POWER Thought #43

"If constructive thoughts are planted positive outcomes will be the result. Plant the seeds of failure and failure will follow." (Sidney Madwed). Think positive, speak positive, and believe fully in your ability to succeed. It WILL happen!

POWER Thought #44

Start the journey, experiment, make strides, struggle through uncertainty, work hard, learn from failures, grow, face fears, overcome challenges, eliminate doubt, serve others, implement change. Do whatever it takes but NEVER GIVE UP!

POWER Thought #45

When you finally discover your passion and purpose it will keep nudging you until you pay attention. Even when you want to turn your back on it, it won't leave you alone. Stop ignoring it!

POWER Thought #46

If you've goals and dreams have become rusty because you've put them on the back shelf for so long, simply take out your polishing cloth and polish-up the talents, gifts, tools, skills and resources you already have until you can see your dream shining again. Refocus on your vision and recommit to yourself!

POWER Thought #47

Your greatest responsibility is to continue growing and reaching new ceilings that allow you to live your most rewarding life and in turn become an inspiration for others to do the same. Lead by example! Commit to fulfilling your purpose. There are those waiting to benefit from what you have to offer. Don't rob them of the blessing!

POWER Thought #48

When doors of opportunity open, walk through them. There is no guarantee that the door will be open again. Recognize priceless opportunities to grow and be fearless enough to GO FOR IT!

POWER Thought #49

Being FEARLESS does not mean you are void of fear... it means you are bold enough, brave enough, and daring enough to pursue the things you want in the presence of fear. Are you demonstrating how fearless you are in life by going for what you want even when the circumstances mount up against you?

POWER Thought #50

Just when you feel you "can't", re-shift your thinking to say "I can and I will." Develop the perseverance, determination, and motivation to keep pushing forward.

POWER Thought #51

When you stop to analyze your skills, talents, experiences, and creativity, recognize that your gifts are incomparable to anyone else and what's destined for you is destined for you. No matter how many people are already doing what you want to do, no matter how fearful you are about whether or not it will fail, no matter what level of education you have, no matter your background or your financial status... if it's meant for you, it will happen! Embark upon your vision of success without letup.

POWER Thought #52

Life is always about choices. The choice is yours to open yourself to possibilities and opportunities that come with taking risks to pursue your dreams or the alternative – choosing to "exist" void of experiencing the true meaning of "living". Make the smart choice.

POWER Thought #53

Once you realize that YOU are the "secret formula" to your success, you can get to work and stop seeking validation from others.

POWER Thought #54

If you are sitting and waiting for a miracle to happen to experience the success you desire you will continue waiting. Those who experience growth, movement, and success are the individuals who step into action and put in the hard work to make it happen. Which category do you fall under?

POWER Thought #55

Instead of attempting to be all things, connect with other talented people who support your mission and vision. When you combine your unique greatness with others who are like-minded you will reach a new level of success.

POWER Thought #56

Ignite your "FEARLESS Factor" to become the best version of YOU. You hold the power!

POWER Thought #57

Work hard to develop the mental posture for success. Start believing that you have everything it takes to soar. It's a daily mental journey and requires daily self-encouragement, self-motivation, and positive self-talk. But once you are convinced of it your power to create the reality you want, you will never make a U-Turn.

POWER Thought #58

Allow yourself to enter each new day filled with purpose to accomplish SOMETHING and to be enthusiastic about each day, each moment, each step towards achieving something new and improved in your life. The miniature moments in life oftentimes go unacknowledged but are often the greatest moments of self-discovery and purpose!

POWER Thought #59

There's no such thing as failure – only lessons learned. Face your fears head on to discover what you're capable of accomplishing. Embrace the enlightening side of every new thing you stretch yourself to do and remain humble enough to accept where you need to make improvements. Successful people aren't perfect, they simply make improvements along their journey.

POWER Thought #60

The world is full of people with great ideas who never reach their dream – not because they don't have what it takes, but because they don't implement what it takes. You say you want success? Then prepare yourself to keep going when others quit, to strive harder when others remain complacent, to find ways to keep yourself motivated when others allow their energy to drain, to speak up when others remain quiet, to serve when others are waiting to be served, to step into what brings you the most fear when others back down. Those who reach success are those who tell themselves every day, "I think I can," until it eventually becomes "I know I can".

POWER Thought #61

No matter what's happening to cause stagnation in your life you can put a halt to the hindrances and devise a new plan, or follow a detour to a new route. The only thing not allowed is giving up!

POWER Thought #62

Fear is the strongest emotion you can experience. Your fear can breed doubt, inadequacy and inactivity but action will breed confidence, momentum and movement. The decision is yours!

POWER Thought #63

Success is non-existent without sacrifice. As you travel the road to pursue your dreams, the sacrifice will sometimes be so great and so frequent that you might ask yourself, "why am I doing this?" Don't allow temporary disappointments, setbacks, or challenges to alter your journey. Don't stop pushing, don't stop moving, don't stop fighting for what you want. Reenergize your spirit to win and when challenges arise, repeat to yourself, "I have everything it takes to overcome this challenge and I'm willing to sacrifice to get to my big reward."

POWER Thought #64

As you strive for success, there will be tests and personality clashes. In some situations a response is required, at other times silence is golden. No matter what, always think before you speak and let your words be supportive, uplifting, and encouraging to others instead of tearing others down with your personal views and opinions.

POWER Thought #65

Invest in your maintenance! When preparing for a road trip you invest in the maintenance of your vehicle because you EXPECT to arrive at your destination. Similarly, EXPECT to arrive at your destination in life and support that expectation by doing the necessary maintenance. Just as you get the oil changed, replace the spark plugs, and refill the windshield wiper fluid – remember to invest in books and learning materials, conferences and workshops, and a coach or mentor who will guide you along your journey. Maintenance will prevent unnecessary breakdowns on your road to success.

POWER Thought #66

Put on your creative thinking cap and intentionally figure out how to achieve your vision of success instead of giving power to the things that threaten your ability to succeed. Claim or reclaim your power!

POWER Thought #67

Instead of throwing a blanket over your mistakes and failures, uncover them, dissect them and learn from them. Allow your mistakes and failures to produce a wiser, better equipped, more knowledgeable individual who is courageous enough to try again. "Only those who dare to fail greatly can ever achieve greatly." (Senator Robert F. Kennedy)

POWER Thought #68

Don't be afraid to inspire someone else to want to achieve great things! Do what you do well and embrace it when others watch you and are moved to action because of your example. Just as you have mentors, coaches and role models whose success you aspire to replicate, as you soar, avoid being offended when others follow your model. And remember that no one can do what you do the way you do it so just keep inspiring others to greatness knowing you are making an impact. It's called an ABUNDANCE mindset. So, who have you inspired today?

POWER Thought #69

Instead of becoming consumed and overwhelmed with the BIG, long-term goals that seem unattainable, focus on the immediate and short-term goals you can achieve to get closer to the BIG goals.

POWER Thought #70

Success lies in your ability to recognize that there is a solution to every challenge you face. Instead of becoming overwhelmed by challenges, successful people FIND SOLUTIONS and stay the course! Keep fighting for what you want and achieve the success you desire.

POWER Thought #71

Are you preventing yourself from living your dreams and creating the reality you want because you feel "secure" where you are right now? Life does not offer guarantees which means your "security" can come crashing down around you at any time. Instead of being stagnant in your life because you feel secure, take some risks, go for the GUSTO, and claim control of your life, your future and your destiny!

POWER Thought #72

Every day you are credited with 86,400 seconds of time to spend as you wish. You can invest your time wisely and put it to good use or you can blow it. Similar to money you withdraw from a bank account, once it's gone its gone! You cannot rewind or go back in time so be strategic about how and where you spend your most valuable asset!

POWER Thought #73

In life, whenever you begin to think your circumstances are worthy of complaint, remember there is always someone with a story more heart wrenching, someone whose system of support is weaker, someone with struggles more desperate, or someone experiencing pain that is greater. Be sure to count your blessings every day and think twice before you start to complain. In every situation there is always something to be grateful for.

POWER Thought #74

Successful people practice seeing the realization of their dream in their mind long before the dream comes to fruition. You can't achieve your dream if you don't visualize it and know clearly what it looks like. Make time to gain clarity of exactly what your picture of success looks like for you without comparison to anyone else's vision.

POWER Thought #75

Don't give up on your dream – fight for it! Eliminate what does not or has not worked and find what does work. Be relentless in pushing, persisting, and persevering until the dream is a reality!!

POWER Thought #76

GREATNESS is a part of your DNA. But have you acknowledged it lately or do you skip all around it? If you don't acknowledge and believe you possess GREATNESS that others deserve to benefit from, how can you expect anyone else to see it, recognize it, or believe it? Stop hanging on the fence and wondering if you have GREATNESS and, instead, walk in it without apologies.

POWER Thought #77

The only opportunity missed is one not pursued. Go after what you want, speak up boldly about your goals and dreams, and put in the work to pursue it. Live on purpose!

POWER Thought #78

The best person to imitate is YOU! Be original, Be authentic, Be unique. Don't be a Carbon-Copy. Stand strong in the greatness with which you are uniquely designed.

POWER Thought #79

"Setbacks are setups for comebacks."
(Willie Jolley). On your journey to
success don't grow weary because of
temporary setbacks. Allow the setbacks
to make you more determined,
persistent, and committed to stepping
into your true purpose and your true
calling. Now is the time to BOLDLY
claim your success, no matter what!!!

POWER Thought #80

Positive affirmations are brief, optimistic statements targeted at a specific subconscious set of beliefs. Positive affirmations keep you focused on your goals and remind you to consciously connect your words and thoughts to those goals. What have you decided you want for your life? Once you know what it is, create and repeat positive affirmations about achieving the goal and claim it before it ever happens. What is your affirmation for today?

POWER Thought #81

Time is a valuable asset. Don't waste it and don't allow others to rob you of it. Every day, get something done that puts you one step closer to your personal, professional, or entrepreneurial dreams. Time won't stand still and wait for you to make up your mind to live your life to its fullest. The only thing time will do is allow you to look back and smile on what you've accomplished OR regret what you were too fearful to explore. Treat your time like a precious gem that cannot be replaced!

POWER Thought #82

Complacency will cause you to miss out on life. Instead of becoming complacent, remind yourself to come off of autopilot and LIVE. Don't allow fears, doubts, or what-ifs to stifle your progress towards living your dreams. Show your true appreciation for life by using every breath in your body and ounce of energy you have to create new possibilities.

POWER Thought #83

"You miss 100% of the shots you don't take." (Wayne Gretzky). How can you expect to achieve greatness or success if you never take the shot? Stop thinking about it and do it!

POWER Thought #84

How you CHOOSE to focus your energy often determines the direction of your day. Instead of frowning and exerting negative energy on what you have not accomplished in your life, smile and hold your head up high about all that you have accomplished by means of your unique talents, gifts, hard work, and persistence. Creating a positive shift in your energy can create positive change!

POWER Thought #85

Don't Give Up Your Dream!! There is someone who is extremely successful today who was, at some point, right where you are at this moment – feeling stuck in life, having limited connections and little financial resources, having great ideas but unsure of how to see them through, passionate about their dream but not sure how it was going to come to fruition – the key is to keep believing in your dream and never lose your commitment to making it happen even when you don't know "how."

POWER Thought #86

Be Optimistic! Optimism is all about attitude… and attitude dictates your progression towards your goals. Focus on your goal, create your blueprint, and activate a positive approach for not allowing anything to stop you from making it happen!!

POWER Thought #87

Those who press onward with their dreams during times when others would give up -- because it's too hard, it's too much time, it's too much work, it's too much sacrifice -- are those who go on to achieve success. Don't stop because it gets challenging along the way. Stay the course!

POWER Thought #88

It's okay to want to achieve more in life, but always remember to stop and express appreciation for what you have, what you've already accomplished, and how far you've come. Never underestimate the value of what you bring to the table JUST AS YOU ARE... with a commitment to becoming even better as you reach higher heights.

POWER Thought #89

There will always be things in life you can't control. When you find yourself against a wall and can't control a situation, simply smile and focus on the things you can control. All things pass, and it's not the situation but your response to the situation that teaches you the greatest life lessons.

POWER Thought #90

Make today a day of REASONS not excuses -- reasons to succeed, reasons to accomplish what you set your mind to do, reasons to think positively, reasons to be resourceful and creative as you control your destiny, reasons to live outside the box and take risks to get what you want. Excuses = Regression whereas Reasons = Progression!

POWER Thought #91

"Courage is what it takes to stand up and speak; courage is also what it takes to sit down and listen." (Winston Churchill). As you pursue your personal vision of success it's just as important to remain teachable and willing to listen as it is to speak up about your goals and dreams. What have you listened to and learned lately?

POWER Thought #92

Never say Never – Always keep the possibilities open when it comes to living your dreams. Create the opportunities, put in the work to make the opportunities successful, and establish a reputation of being the person who people want to extend opportunities to. You have what it takes!

POWER Thought #93

During your journey of development and growth, expect that some people will understand and some won't, some will support and some you expect to support won't. Don't become discouraged. Life is about change and not everyone will know how to embrace the changes you are making. Keep an open mind for all the new, positive changes life will bring your way.

POWER Thought #94

At some point, you must stop looking outside of YOU for the answers. All the answers lie within you. Your mind, your thoughts, your patterns, your behavior, your actions produce the results you want for your life. It's time to find the greatness within and start achieving the success you have been searching for!

POWER Thought #95

"Mind over matter." Your mind is a powerful tool that has the ability to control you, persuade you, motivate you, or hinder you. Make up your mind to walk the talk, pursue your goals, and finish what you start.

POWER Thought #96

SPEAK UP about your goals. Tell others what you want to accomplish and don't be afraid to ask for help. Asking for help doesn't mean you're weak, it means you're strong enough to recognize that success is not achieved as an island all to yourself. Allow others to experience the joy of helping you accomplish your goals and dreams!

POWER Thought #97

Dare to do something different towards achieving one of your goals today!

POWER Thought #98

Every day, take a moment to look in the mirror and reflect on the person beyond the reflection. What defines you? What makes you beautiful on the inside? What makes you strong and courageous? How are you demonstrating boldness to live your best life? Delving beyond the reflection will help you to gain clarity in your life and determine how to progress instead of standing still.

POWER Thought #99

If you don't accomplish something today, it's okay. Don't give up on your goal because you fall off track. Sometimes you simply need to regroup, refocus, and reenergize. A minor setback does not have to mean complete failure. Dust yourself off and continue in your journey!

POWER Thought #100

Struggle and Success go hand-in-hand. Struggle pushes you to work harder to achieve success; Success helps you to appreciate the struggles you endured to achieve it. Don't despise the struggles you have to endure to grow in your journey.

POWER Thought #101

Repetition is a powerful tool in taking control of your destiny. Engage in repetitive, positive self-talk on a daily basis and reassure yourself: "I deserve the best. I have what it takes to create the life I desire for myself. I will not give up until I cross the finish line".

POWER Thought #102

Without change you cannot experience the joys of growth, progress, and achievement. And you would never experience the comeback from adversity, disappointment, and failure. The more you grow as a person the more you will experience change. Embrace change and allow it to make you a more balanced and well-rounded person.

POWER Thought #103

Focused, driven, determined, motivated, committed, positive, passionate, teachable, humble, authentic, confident, courageous, bold, savvy and assertive – these are a few pieces of the puzzle for achieving success. Routinely conduct a self-assessment to determine if you possess each of these characteristics as you pursue your dreams.

POWER Thought #104

The time has come to WAKE UP and ELIMINATE EXCUSES in order to make your dreams come true. The difference between those who live their dreams and those who simply daydream is the willingness to step into action. Dreams only come true when you are committed to the dream, create a plan to achieve the dream, and put work into making the dream happen. Put in the work and experience the rewards!

POWER Thought #105

"Commitment leads to action. Action brings your dream closer" (Marcia Wieder). Are you committed to taking the action necessary to see your dreams come true? Action means actively putting in the work to create opportunities, develop new relationships, and persevering when things seem impossible. Commitment goes a step further than determination. When you are committed you stay true to the course of action you are on and don't allow anything to stop you!

POWER Thought #106

As long as you are living and breathing, you can learn and grow in life and in the pursuit of your dreams. Never develop the mentality that you have all the answers. At times, just listening and observing will help you flourish by leaps and bounds!

POWER Thought #107

Dismiss the word IMPOSSIBLE from your thought process. Anything you can dream and believe is within your reach. "Impossible is just a big word thrown around by those who find it easier to live the world they've been given than to explore the power they have to change it. Impossible is not a declaration. Impossible is potential" (Adidas). Dare yourself to live beyond the impossible!

POWER Thought #108

Passion is the thing that nurtures your spirit, the thing you would do even if no one paid you to do it, the thing that makes you feel alive and exhilarated because of the limitless opportunities it offers. Find, pursue and enjoy your passion. When you pursue your passion you begin to experience the true definition of living!

POWER Thought #109

Never allow the word "NO" to discourage you from achieving your life goals. In the process of working to live your dreams, even if you hear the word "NO" a thousand times just recognize that you have nothing to fear because "NO" simply means NEXT OPPORTUNITY.

POWER Thought #110

You're not meant to look like the person beside you, you're not meant to possess the talents and skills of the person in front of you, you're not meant to live the life of the person behind you. You are uniquely designed and possess an individualized greatness. Accept it, embrace it, and never compare yourself to anyone else.

POWER Thought #111

Transformation is a three-fold process –
it begins with your thoughts and a
mindset that you can achieve anything,
which in turn affects your words that
speak life to your goals, aspirations and
dreams, finalized by execution for
realizing your dreams. Believe It, Speak
It, Execute It!

POWER Thought #112

Don't be afraid to share your greatness
with the world. Each person is created
with a unique set of gifts and talents
designed to serve and help others. Show
boldness and courage as you express
those gifts and bless someone else with
your greatness.

POWER Thought #113

At the root of a strong, empowered individual are strong, healthy and stable relationships. Healthy relationships are built upon a foundation of mutual honor, respect, trust, integrity, and communication. Any relationship that does not exude these characteristics will make you feel unsteady, unstable, and anxious instead of uplifted, motivated, and focused. Periodically evaluate the relationships (platonic and non-platonic) in your life and confirm the foundation and mutual feelings that those relationships are built upon.

POWER Thought #114

Take the GOLDEN Oath: "I am intently focused on living my life like it's GOLDEN. I will allow my actions to reflect that I am making the most of each day, I will celebrate my accomplishments and learn from my mistakes, I will not allow negativity to enter my world for more than 60-seconds without dismissing it, I will make time to stop and smell the roses, I will reflect on how blessed I am even when I am experiencing challenges or struggles in my life, and I will focus on the fact that life is what I make it and that my life DESERVES to be GOLDEN"!

POWER Thought #115

Say "YES" to you. If you're always saying YES to everyone else but always saying "NO" to yourself, you need to make a shift. Eliminate saying NO to setting aside "me time" despite all the ripping and running you do for everyone else, NO to pampering yourself and making yourself feel special on the inside and outside, NO to investing in your personal development and growth. The time has come for the NO's to take a seat. Say YES to you today, you deserve it!!

POWER Thought #116

Surround yourself with those who believe in you, support you, applaud you, and celebrate you. Having a positive inner circle of individuals who help to keep you grounded, who offer constructive criticism, who provide positive reinforcement and accountability, and who lend their support in your endeavors is key for achieving success.

POWER Thought #117

Today is the day to step up to the plate and hit the ball out of the park! Stop sitting on your dreams, stop thinking about how wonderful it would be to achieve your dreams… and START ACTING ON YOUR DREAMS. Every accomplished dream begins with an empowered, focused, determined individual who creates an action plan and takes steps towards seeing the dream come to fruition. It is never too late! Start Now!

POWER Thought #118

Your energy says it all! When you walk into a room does your energy announce you as a positive, empowered and happy individual or does your energy announce you as a negative, pessimistic and arrogant individual? Your energy is what attracts people to you. If you want to attract the most positive, empowered, supportive, and uplifting people into your inner circle then that is what you yourself must reflect. Every day presents a new opportunity to redirect your energy towards attracting positivity into your life.

POWER Thought #119

When things are looking down you can
choose to sulk, complain, moan and
groan… OR you can choose to create a
plan of action. One guarantee: if you
continue to sulk, complain, moan and
groan things will remain the same. But
if you create and implement a plan of
action things are bound to change. Take
control of your life and starting working
on your plan!

POWER Thought #120

What time is it? It's time to put your knowledge to action, time to become empowered to live your best life now, time to stop putting off until tomorrow what you can do today, time to transform your life into the life you deserve and desire, time to set aside all fears and doubts, and time to display boldness, audacity and determination as someone who refuses to settle for less!

POWER Thought #121

Run towards the goals in your life that scare you the most; pray for the people who are watching and hoping that you fail; and become stronger and more determined by the challenges you have to endure and overcome.

POWER Thought #122

If you really want to get to your intended destination, don't become distracted by what anyone else is doing. Focus on the necessary action steps that will get you closer to YOUR goals. Don't compete with anyone else, Don't compare yourself to anyone else, and Don't try to imitate anyone else. Success is not a race and it's not a competition. Put on "blinders" and walk confidently in your lane.

POWER Thought #123

Success is not earned in a single triumph but in an untold number of feats!! Instead of trying to avoid falling down on your path to success... be the person who falls down, gets up quickly, dusts off, and tries again until you achieve what you want. Failure only comes to those who stop trying – it's always a choice.

POWER Thought #124

What's holding you back? Stop waiting for the perfect moment. Stop playing the When/Then Game. Stop asking "why" and ask "why not". What have you given yourself permission to pursue or accomplish without explanations or excuses?

POWER Thought #125

When you play in a zone that's small, safe and familiar, you have to expect small, safe and familiar results. When you step up your game and play in a zone where you take risks and do things you've never done before, you can expect new, different and bigger results than you've ever had before!

POWER Thought #126

Developing a success mindset is not a one-shot task…. it's an ongoing project! You must wake up every single day ready to talk yourself through whatever it takes to stay on course. Your mind must be MADE UP to WIN! Your thoughts must motivate you to keep going instead of giving up. Your willpower begins internally with your mindset and will carry you through for the long-haul!

POWER Thought #127

Your story has power! Don't discount your story and the meaning it can have for someone else. And don't compare your story -- what you have or have not accomplished and the weight it carries -- to anyone else's story in determining whether or not you should tell it. Instead, share your story with authenticity and passion as often as possible. Telling your story is a part of creating your legacy!

POWER Thought #128

Enter every situation, circumstance, relationship, friendship, partnership, or collaboration with higher expectations of yourself than the other person and you will always receive great reward.

POWER Thought #129

When you see everyone going in one direction, have the audacity to go and explore in the opposite direction – that's the definition of a Trailblazer! Be FEARLESS enough to pursue new, creative and innovative ideas that separate you from everyone else.

POWER Thought #130

The moment you stop allowing your internal fears and the opinions of others to cause you to minimize your unique gift, is the moment you're able to start uncovering your real purpose, walking in your truth, and making an impact.

POWER Thought #131

If you want it bad enough call again, ask again, send another email, make another visit, mail another postcard, write another letter... Success comes to those who don't accept NO as the final answer. Keep asking until you hear YES!

POWER Thought #132

Always stay true to your character, no
matter what, so people never have to
second-guess what to expect when they
befriend you, hire you, partner with you,
or refer you.

POWER Thought #133

Just because you want success doesn't mean you will always have the right answers, doesn't mean you will always feel like doing the work, and doesn't mean you will always have support from the people who have the resources to help you. Your path to succeeding is about having a hunger that outweighs all opposition and staying in a mode of ACTION even when you internally feel stuck! Keep your foot on the gas pedal, not the brakes.

POWER Thought #134

There is no smooth road to success. If it was easy everyone would do it. Develop the willpower to decide what you want and never stop until you get it.

POWER Thought #135

Don't allow people without a vision tell you that you can't achieve yours. With God's backing and the support from a "tribe" of people who believe in you, ANYTHING IS POSSIBLE. Don't back down, Don't slow down, Don't minimize your dream. Go out and get your blessings.

POWER Thought #136

Show Up the way you want to be viewed. If you want to be viewed as a person who is serious about achieving your goals show up on time (preferably early), show up enthusiastic about what you do, show up willing to listen more than you talk, and show up ready to give before you ask.

POWER Thought #137

There is no "undo" or "delete" button as you travel your journey to success, so stop losing sleep over the mistakes you've made, the failures you've experienced, and what didn't work out. Instead, spend your time and energy focused on the many possibilities and the potential in front of you. Moving forward requires looking forward!

POWER Thought #138

Pursue the goals that enhance your growth and eliminate the non-essential "stuff" that hinders it, sacrifice what you "want" to do for the things you "need" to do to succeed, approach every obstacle as a reason to persist instead of a crutch that keeps you stagnate, find another way instead of giving up when things don't go as planned. You will only achieve success if you focus, decide, act, persist, roll with the punches, and never give up!

POWER Thought #139

One thought, One idea, One step… is all it takes to begin creating a new life for yourself. But the question remains: Are you bold enough to make the first move?

POWER Thought #140

To get what you want, you have to know what you want. To know what you want you have to clearly identify it by writing it down. Any goal or ambition not written down is just a wish. Take out your note pad and pen and start writing about the reality you want to create for your life.

POWER Thought #141

Fear often presents itself in the form of procrastination. Procrastinating on making moves to accomplish a goal because you fear you aren't good enough, you fear you don't have as much knowledge as someone else, you fear criticism, or you fear rejection... so you keep putting it off. Being successful comes with the knowledge that there are no guarantees. So, instead of procrastinating -- Act now, Fail now, Learn now so you can discover what works, implement, and move on to greater goals.

POWER Thought #142

Take your God-given gifts seriously and never underestimate how deeply it can bless someone else's life AND how that blessing can come back to be a blessing to you.

POWER Thought #143

Anything that will hinder your growth should be of NO INTEREST to you. Only permit the people and things that support your growth to stay on your radar.

POWER Thought #144

Everything is not meant for everyone. Don't get sidetracked by the "hype" of what everyone else is doing. Stop and make sure your dreams and the work you're putting in align with YOUR vision of success. It is much more rewarding, fulfilling and enjoyable to run your own race at your own pace.

POWER Thought #145

The Sky Is The Limit… but only if you're willing to lift your head and look up!

POWER Thought #146

If you don't believe it, don't expect anyone else to believe it. The one thing that must remain consistent in your journey is your confidence and belief in where you are headed. Do not allow anyone or anything to deter your belief that IT WILL happen... No if's, and's, or but's about it.

POWER Thought #147

Your success depends on your willingness to frequently assess what you've been doing, acknowledge what you need to change, and execute to change it!

POWER Thought #148

Encourage, uplift, or support someone else without any expectations and watch how much faster you will get to you own destination!

POWER Thought #149

Become a reflection of what you want in your life. If you want peace, calm, contentment, fulfillment, joy, and sense of purpose

POWER Thought #150

Each day amidst the hustle, bustle, and grind to achieve your goals, stop to take a few deep breaths and find JOY in your life and what's already in front of you. JOY has the power to transition your sweat and tears for getting what you want into fulfillment and purpose. Find JOY knowing your journey and every step you take has meaning.

ABOUT THE AUTHOR

Enthusiastic. Engaging. Innovative.

Cheryl Wood is one of the most compelling thought leaders and voices in motivational speaking today. Armed with a mission to empower, Cheryl has impacted the lives of thousands through her life-changing principles of FEARLESS living. She is an award-winning entrepreneur, speaker, author, and business coach who specializes in equipping audiences to stretch their thinking, expand their expectations, and play a bigger game. She compels individuals to embrace their personal power to visualize and achieve their desired success. Her enthusiasm for thriving in life is contagious and sparks a flame among audiences to boldly step outside of their comfort zone, take calculated risks, and remove self-limiting beliefs to reach their greatest potential.

Cheryl's personal story of taking a leap of faith to transition from the frustrated mother of three who was "existing" to the mission-driven woman pursuing her passion and living in her purpose resonates with men and women globally. She authentically shares the ups and downs of her journey from a successful career to launching a small t-shirt business in her basement to growing an international speaking and coaching business that allows her to transform lives. Cheryl's message equally empowers leaders, career professionals, executives, and entrepreneurs to persist until they reach their goals even in the face of challenges, fears, and setbacks.

Cheryl has received numerous awards and recognition for her work including 2012 Forty Under 40 Small Business Honoree, Prince George's County Social Innovation Fund; 2012 Inspirational Entrepreneur of the Year Award, Stiletto Woman in Business; 2011 Small Business Influencer Award, Small Business Technology; 2010 Business Woman of the Year Award, The Professional Black Woman; 2010 Entrepreneurial Spirit Award, Morgan State University; and 2010 Governor's Citation for Excellence in Small Business.

For more information:
Visit www.cherylwoodempowers.com
Contact: info@cherylwoodempowers.com

CPSIA information can be obtained at www.ICGtesting.com
Printed in the USA
BVOW08s0139150813

328510BV00007B/19/P

9 781467 581240